I0069949

Digital Dollars

10 Ways To Make Money Online

DINASTY BROWN

© 2020

Introduction

Introduction

43% of people in the US are working from home or making money online.

The number of people who have been granted the privilege to work from home has increased by 159% within the past 8 years due to:

- 💲 Advancement in technology
- 💲 Growth of the online economy
- 💲 Convenience for employers and lower overhead cost

Out of 43% of those working from home, 1 out of 4 people work for themselves and are going digital some way.

CNBC News reported, "People who work from home earn more than those who commute." The reason for this is most work-from-home jobs are based on production or commission, not labor. The 10 ways I'll be outlining to make money online from home do not require you to "physically" go to work in any way. You'll learn how to stop trading your time and effort for money, also what satisfies me most, there's no cap on how much you can make. This is why typically people who work from home online make more than people who work at a job on an hourly wage.

So, if you are reading this book I'm going to guess that you are either looking to work for yourself or find a way where you'll be able to work from home. For a lot of aspiring entrepreneurs, the ultimate goal is to achieve BOTH, and I am here to help you learn how.

My entrepreneurship journey began during my freshman year in college when I was 18. Now I've always had a job since I was legally allowed to work, I'm not one to sit around broke and hey I like nice things. But the hassle of getting up, going to someone's job, it takes up a huge chunk of my day and at the end of the week your only reward is a small paycheck that's just enough to get you by, I knew something had to give. That wasn't the life for me and I'm guessing because you have begun reading this book it's not for you as well.

At 18 in college I was so broke I didn't have enough money to wash my clothes, but I also was a full-time student, taking over 15 credit hours a semester so I didn't have the time to work for anyone. Trust me I tried, this led me to a part-time job at McDonald's and yes the stereotype is true, that's legit the worst job ever. But to make matters worse I had to work the overnight shift because class was during the day, this took away my "homework" time and late-night study session along with I was oversleeping and missing my 8 AM lecture every other day. So it was either work for McDonald's or fail school, at this time school was the priority.

If you can see already, I'm just like you and just like you, I was on social media admiring and being inspired by so many digital entrepreneur's success. I mean it was people my age and look just like me becoming millionaires by selling things and making money online. Why the hell couldn't I do it, it must be easy right??? Guess what, it was. Within a week I set up an Instagram store, found a supplier, connected a payment processor and business email and before you knew it I had my first e-commerce store. That store made over 6-figures in 6-months.

I had showed and proved to myself that "work" didn't have to interfere with my life. I didn't have to cancel things or simply not live life on my terms because of a job. By employing myself and making money online I set my own schedule, made my own money, and created my own life. And I'm sure you're ready to do the same.

So whether you are seeking to "make money online", get some "sleep coin", "make money in your sleep", "run a business from your iPhone", "work from home", gain "Wi-Fi money", and now my new saying, collect them "digital dollars" this book is for you and you're in the right place!

I'm going to share with you my Top 10 ways of making money online, all of these businesses can be run from the comfort of your home and by using your phone. If you're ready flip the page, get out a pen, and let's get started.

Affiliate Marketing

Chapter 1. Affiliate Marketing

Definition - Affiliate marketing
a marketing arrangement by which an online retailer pays a commission to an external website for traffic or sales generated from its referrals.

Let's start with the most basic way to make cash online. Affiliate marketing allows you to earn a living by promoting other's brands. By becoming an affiliate marketer with a company or brand, referring their product or service, you are rewarded with a commission. Basically, you'll earn a percentage of their sales just by sharing a link or code. There are several digital entrepreneurs who are affiliates full time. Business woman Tatiana James is known for making $20,000 a month with affiliate marketing. So yes, this can be a real career for you!

In my experience affiliate marketing works best if you have built a strong personal brand or platform. For example, if you have a fashion blog that gets thousands to millions of views or a YouTube channel which we'll later discuss, and you are a verified resource for your audience. It works best to partner with multiple clothing companies and fashion brands that provide perks for wearing their items and share these finds with your viewers. Drive the traffic to your affiliate link, and BOOM you make cash.

Here are some companies that are known to have some of the top affiliate programs and great pay.

$ BH Cosmetics

$ HubSpot

- 💲 Amazon
- 💲 Shopify
- 💲 Nordstrom

Some people may think, why would I promote someone else's company and I want to create my own. I'm not here to discourage you or even recommend that you don't have or own your own business. But we are all only one person and we can't do and make everything ourselves. We promote and refer other brands daily, without even noticing. Think about the last time someone asked you, where did you get that shirt or OMG you lost so much weight how? Now imagine instead of referring the business you got it from or sending them to the company website for free, you provide them with a simple affiliate code and you're paid 30% commission of the sale each time someone asks. I mean you are sending them to another company anyway, you might as well get paid for it. It's much more simple, easy to manage and a low investment. Also, you're able to add other products to your business without having to create the product yourself. This saves time, money, headache and responsibility.

Most companies have simple affiliate applications or requirements to begin earning commissions through them. Pay ranges from 5%-75% of sales for each customer you refer by using your link or code to purchase. For example, I offer a 70% commission to clients who refer my course to other business owners.Both of my Online Masterclasses have affiliate programs that have an added bonus for my clients to earn more money and have an additional income to invest in their business. The only requirement is to be enrolled in the course. Once enrolled I activate everyone's affiliate link and payout 70% commission of all sales. So if my client would like to share with a peer or friend the experience of taking my online course and that friend is interested in signing up. They simply just have to share their affiliate link, the person purchases, and my client receives 70% of the purchase price to their PayPal. Yes, it's that simple, this is why starting with affiliate marketing is easy and a quick way to make cash online.

Let's break this down into numbers so that you're able to see the earning potential.

💲 **Course Purchase Price = $500**

💲 **70% of $500 = $350**

💲 **Refer 10 people a month and earn = $3500**

If earning an additional $3500 a month from literally sharing a website link sounds good to you, I suggest you continue reading. We are just getting started!

RESOURCES

Websites to find the best paying affiliate programs:

Affiliate Unguru | www.affiliateunguru.com

Affiliate UNguru is a site where you can find honest and helpful reviews, along with actionable tips on starting your own online business.

Flex Offers | www.flexoffers.com

FlexOffers is an affiliate network that connects you to many reputable brand name companies who you can become an affiliate for

CJ Affiliate | www.CJ.com

CJ Affiliate an affiliate marketplace, where you can find thousands of products to promote and make money

Affiliate Marketing Mastery | www.affiliatemarketingmastery.co

Learn from Stefan James, a 7-figure internet entrepreneur, life and business coach

PLAN OF ACTION

List 3 Companies you genuinely love and would like to become an affiliate of.

1 _____

2 _____

3 _____

Visit their website or email the owner and seek out information on any affiliate or referral they may have. Good luck and happy earning!

> I will make $_____ in the next _____ months by selling _____ of _____ for $_____.

NOTES:

_____

_____

_____

_____

_____

_____

Braindump

Course Creation

Chapter 2: Course Creation

Definition - Course Creation
the content and promotional planning process by which [someone creates] learning products and experiences are designed, developed, and delivered.

It is projected that by 2022, the online course market will reach over $275 billion. Online teaching and digital learning grow up to 30% each year. There are so many experts, gurus, and coaches offering their knowledge online in course form. I personally love it, and this is my main source of income. Nothing beats digital marketing. Think about it, one course can make you millions of dollars. Depending on your style of teaching, you could have created that course in one day and it pays you for life.

- **$** **Live Webinar:** A webinar is an online meeting or presentation held via the Internet in real-time

- **$** **Evergreen or Pre-Recorded Webinar:** a pre-recorded video, set on auto-play, with custom call-to-actions for engagement

- **$** **Group Coaching:** a process of helping individuals within the group close the gap between the life they are living and the life they would like to live

- **$** **1on1 Training:** Direct and Personal hands-on teaching between you and an individual

($) **Master Classes:** specialty classes in which learning objectives are achieved through in-depth practice accompanied by detailed instruction

($) **Online Course:** an onetime course conducted over the internet

You can find online courses that teach anything from cooking to marketing or even dating and self-confidence. You can obtain knowledge or "know-how" to something people want to learn. The basics of course creation is simply packaging that knowledge in video, written, or audio form to sell at a set price.

This package of knowledge can be delivered instantly through video playbacks, private link videos on YouTube or Google Drive or you can upload your content into a course creation hosting platform.

Here is some of the top course creation host at this time:

($) **Thinkific**

($) **Kajabi**

($) **Kartra**

($) **Samscart**

Along with these platforms that'll sell and host your course for you, you can try Skillshare or Udemy. If you'd like to check out Skillshare, they are offering two months FREE! Use Coupon Code: igamb4587.

You also can hold your courses or classes at a later date or live. My business model is split up 50/50. I do live classes typically to launch a new course using Webinar Jam. For smaller classes or if you're just starting, some course creators also use Google Hangouts or Zoom to host live trainings. The other half of my courses are pre-recorded, packaged together, and sold as a masterclass. I typically use Teachable to host masterclasses and single online courses are sold separately on my website as a digital product.

What is the earning potential with course creation? It ranges from a few thousand to millions. My first course launch "Young Boss Boot Camp" sold $3,200 the first day.

To date, my most recent and successful course launch has been $50,000 in 30 days.I have seen courses priced very low at $9 and other courses priced extremely high at $9,999. As a creator, you have to be knowledgeable and confident in what you're offering. The price of your training reflects your worth, but it should also reflect what students or attendees will get out of the course. By investing in you, what will they gain in return? Keep this in mind as you are structuring pricing and the components of your course.

Let's do some simple math, we'll use my master class again as an example. The masterclass is $500, let's say in one month 100 people sign up for my online training.

$500x100 students = $50,000

Do you have something you can share or teach that's of value to others? If so your $50K month is closer than you think! Reasons why I love online course creation:

It's a low startup cost, you're able to be yourself and teach what you know, you are legitimately adding value to someone's life, there's no cap on your revenue so earning potential is indefinite, and anyone can do it!

✓ It's a low startup cost
✓ You're able to be yourself and teach what you know
✓ You are legitimately adding value to someone's life
✓ There's no cap on your revenue so earning potential is indefinite
✓ Anyone can do it

It's multiple ways you can launch and promote your course. Some of my favorite ways to close sales are email marketing, online webinars, phone consultations, speaking events, and social media marketing.

Here's how I begin my process and create a course:

1 Outline Why You're Creating The Online Course.

2 Pick An Online Course Topic.

3 Validate Your Online Course.

4 Create Your Course Content.

5 Host Your Online Course.

6 Price Your Online Course.

7 Create A Course Sales Page.

8 Market Your Online Course.

9 Enroll New Students in Course.

10 Provide Additional Support to Ensure Your Students Succeed.

RESOURCES

Teachable | www.teachable.com
Create and sell beautiful online courses with the platform used by the best online entrepreneurs to sell $300m+ to over 18 million students worldwide.

GumRoad | www.GumRoad.com
Gumroad is an online platform that enables creators to sell products directly to consumers.

Webinar Jam | www.WebinarJam.com
Flexible webinar hosting software used by various businesses and industries for online marketing.

Udemy | www.Udemy.com
An online learning and teaching marketplace with over 100000 courses and 24 million students.

Course From Scratch | www.CourseFromScratch.com
Course From Scratch Helps Over 4,000 People Create Courses On Hundreds Of Unique Topics

"
I will make $_____ in the next
____ months by selling ____ of
_____ for $_____.
"

NOTES:

_____

_____

_____

_____

_____

_____

_____

_____

Braindump

Books & E-Books

Chapter 3: Books & E-Books

Definition - E-Book
an electronic version of a printed book that can be read on a computer or handheld device designed specifically for this purpose

Have you ever wanted to write a book? It's a pretty universal goal that everyone thinks of. From my little nieces and nephews to my grandma, they all say, "I want to write a book someday" and I know you guys can't be much different. Similar to course creation, you can package your knowledge, tell a story, or document an aspect of life in written form which can be sold digitally or as a physical copy. Both can easily be sold online and I'm about to teach you how.

Writing a book is easy, you'll want to start with an outline. Just like in school how they taught you before writing an essay. You can grab my "10 Step Guide to Writing Your First Book" outline for free on my website. www.CoachedbyDinasty.com.

✓ Choose a topic that matches your audience's needs.
✓ Outline each chapter of your eBook.
✓ Break down each chapter as you write.
✓ -Design your eBook.
✓ Plan Launch.

I've written 3 books so far and usually what everyone struggles with is actually getting it done. The best advice I've ever received when I started writing my first book in 2015, was to put yourself on a schedule and just WRITE.

Take out 2-3 hours a day, 5-6 days a week, and set those as your writing hours. For me, I'm a night owl so my writing hours are 10-12, I usually go past 12 but those are my hours. Phone off, TV off, laptop on lap and I write. No distractions and everyone around me must respect it. This is how you get it done.

Secondly, just write. Do not try to perfect everything at first. You do not need to go back and make edits and changes when you start. My process is I write a chapter, re-read, make small edits that stick out to me while reading but I don't spend a lot of time on this, I move on to the next chapter. Editing and formatting is your editor's job, not yours. Your job is to WRITE!

BONUS TIP something else that helps me finish was designing the cover early on. Once you get the cover designed it's real, then it becomes visual. You can see it and almost feel it, trust me you'll get your book done for sure after that.

Websites like CreateSpace and Lulu will let you upload and take your book to print without getting a formal publisher involved, and you can even get your book on Amazon.com so people can buy it there. If you are going to take this seriously and would like your book available in multiple stores you'll need to purchase an ISBN. Bowker can assign an International Standard Book Number (ISBN) to your book or eBook (EPUB) making it eligible for distribution to Amazon, Kobo, the iBookstore and the Barnes & Noble Nook store in addition to the Lulu Marketplace. If you plan to write multiple books, purchase the pack of 10, it's a better bargain.

Next, you will need to legally claim and protect your work. To register a book or other creative work, simply go to www.copyright.gov. There is an online portal to register copyrights for photographs, sculptures, and written works. Fill out the form, pay the fee and you are registered.

Let's say you're not a strong writer so you feel like you can't do it. No!That doesn't have to stop you. It's time to learn the power of outsourcing, this is where you work smarter and not harder. Have you heard of a ghostwriter? A ghostwriter is someone whose job it is to write material for someone else who is the named author.

Not only that you can choose to hire a writer for your eBook, a graphic designer to design the cover, or a freelancer to format the eBook for you to help minimize the work you need to put into it. I'll be covering freelancing more in the next chapter.

So let's do the math! It'll only make sense if it makes dollars right? We are going to use my book "Become a Boss" as an example. It took me about 2 weeks to write Become a Boss. On launch day I sold 132 copies at $16.99 each.

132 books x $16.99 = $2,242.68

Not too bad right? Have you made that much in a day just from writing? Doing special promotions and sales on your book also are excellent. For example, the free book plus shipping funnel I launched for "Become a Boss", I give the book away for free and customers paid a $7.99 shipping and handling fee. I sold over 1,000 copies of my book in 48 hours using this method. I didn't make much profit from the actual book sale, but this funnel had a course attached to it where I was able to capitalize and make digital dollars! Now 1,000 more people in the world have access to my book, once they read it naturally they'll be ready to come back for more and the dollars keep coming in. If writing a book has been one of your goals, stop putting it off and go for it! It'll be a source of income for life.

RESOURCES

Amazon KDP | www.kdp.amazon.com
Fast, easy and free way for authors and publishers to keep control and publish their books worldwide on the Kindle

Canva | www.Canva.com
Create any genre of custom ebook designs with Canva's impressively easy to use online ebook creator

CreateSpace | www.CreateSpace.com
On-Demand Publishing, LLC, doing business as CreateSpace, is a self-publishing service owned by Amazon.

Lulu | www.Lulu.com

Make Your Ideas Count - Bring Your Book To Life. Publish For Free.

Urban Writers | www.theurbanwriters.com

A writing service company. They provide written content in all forms. From eBooks to articles to SEO content. Need

Bowker | www.myidentifiers.com

ISBNs from Bowker make your book easier to discover. Great Self-Publisher Tool.

A to Z Book Publishing | www.myidentifiers.com

The company publishes and print on demand books for clients. We also offer ghostwriting services. CoachDinasty code to get a 15% discount off of your coaching, ghostwriting, or publishing services.

PLAN OF ACTION

"

I will make $_____ in the next ____ months by selling ____ of _____ for $_____.

"

NOTES:

_____

_____

_____

_____

_____

Braindump

Freelancer

Chapter 4: Freelancer

Definition - Freelancer
a person who is self-employed and is not necessarily committed to a particular employer long-term.

Are you so good at writing that you can do it for someone else? Do you have talents other than writing or have another online skill set you'd be willing to do for money? It would be a good idea to brand yourself as a freelancer.

As a freelancer, you work as an independent contractor that gets paid for every job you execute. You are not obligated to your clients, and what you do is solely your decision. Make your own pay, work your own hours.

For example, if you're a writer, administrative assistant, graphic designer, teacher, developer, etc., at your 9-5 job, you can take those same skills and find clients online who are looking for it and will pay you.

How long does it take you to respond to all your boss' s emails and return calls in a day? Let's say 4 hours and as a receptionist or assistant, you are getting paid 12/hr. Did you know you can build a profile online as a Virtual Assistant, which we'll cover more in the next chapter, and charge $15-$20 an hour for the same task? But now you're able to do it from the comfort of your home and on your own time and own terms. And a bonus, you can have multiple businesses hire you for the same job. Imagine 5 companies paying you $15 an hour to handle all of their administrative tasks.

The number of people who have been granted the privilege to work from home has increased by 159% within the past 8 years due to:

- (💲) **Writing**
- (💲) **Editing and Proofreading**
- (💲) **Marketing and PR**
- (💲) **Graphic Design**
- (💲) **Online Tutoring**
- (💲) **Transcription**
- (💲) **Data Entry**
- (💲) **Computer & IT**
- (💲) **Virtual Assistance**

As an addition to my coaching and consulting service, I offer freelance services to my clients as well such as creating and managing Facebook ads, developing written marketing plans, and even branding and designing their social media pages. Branding and Designing social media pages are super fun to me! On average I'll receive 7-10 Instagram Makeover requests a week. I charge $150 for the service.

7 Instagram Makeovers X $150 = $1,050

That's an extra thousand a week added to my income by simply designing someone's social media account. Fun and easy money right?!I also hire many freelancers in my business as well. Personally, I have multiple freelancers who are a part of my team. It definitely gets the task done quicker and takes the headache out of managing full time employees. This is why business owners will enjoy hiring you.

There are a few favorite websites of mine I find people to hire.

- ✓ Fiverr
- ✓ Upwork
- ✓ Freelancer
- ✓ Facebook Groups and Marketplace
- ✓ Guru

Freelancers can apply for jobs on specific online writing job boards, but also general freelance websites like the ones listed above.

All allow you to create your own profile where customers can easily see an example of your work and previous client reviews.

To make money online as a freelancer, you need to start by building out a strong portfolio. That may mean doing some free work with some reputable mid-tier brands or small business owners to start. I suggest networking in professional Facebook groups and offer a free trial on your services. Make sure in exchange the customer leaves a review and/or posts their work and experience with you. Once you gain a strong portfolio, you can start reaching out to potential big clients to earn more money online.

Here are your steps to get started:

1 Consider whether freelancing is for you.

2 Find a platform.

3 Build your profile.

4 Determine your price.

5 Build your portfolio.

6 Promote to find work.

RESOURCES

Fiverr | www.Fiverr.com
World's largest freelance marketplace for businesses to focus on growth at an affordable cost.

Upwork | www.Upwork.com
Access a wide range of freelancers to help you with your next business project

Freelancer | www.Freelancer.com
Instant Access To 30M+ Designers, Developers, Writers & More.

One of the best freelance websites to find & hire Freelancers online and get work done.

PLAN OF ACTION

" I will make $_____ in the next _____ months by selling _____ of _____ for $_____. "

NOTES:

_____

_____

_____

_____

_____

_____

_____

_____

Braindump

Social Media Manager
or
Virtual Assistant

Chapter 5: Social Media Manager or Virtual Assistant

Definition - Social Media Manager or Virtual Assistant

individual in an organization trusted with monitoring, contributing to, filtering, measuring and otherwise guiding the social media presence of a brand, product, individual or corporation.

As mentioned in the previous chapter Virtual Assistant work or becoming a Social Media Manager can be very lucrative and fun. Now you can do this as a freelancer, or you can build an entire business and brand. Many agency owners have started as freelancers to gain experience and build their clientele, then gradually build their business. Here we will discuss the business side of things and developing your Social Media Marketing Agency or Virtual Assistant Agency.

The difference is, as a freelancer you are completing a one-time job. When you have an agency you work on ongoing projects, clients typically pay a monthly retainer for management and other administrative tasks to be done regularly.

A virtual assistant (typically abbreviated to VA) is generally self-employed and provides professional administrative, technical, or creative assistance to clients remotely from a home office. Some skills you'll need to have are word processing, oral communication and writing skills, computer skills, self-motivation and discipline, quick thinking and effective decision making.

Lastly, a love for continuous learning. You should always be investing in yourself and the team to learn even more, this will add value for your clients.

With so many businesses operating mostly, or completely online, it's a no brainer that many companies and entrepreneurs hire virtual assistants to help keep them organized and complete day to day office tasks. Virtual assistants are becoming an essential part of running a business. You'll be hired to complete several tasks including but not limited to writing, order processing, bookkeeping, scheduling appointments, social media, and customer support

According to PayScale, virtual assistants make between $10 – $50 per hour, which translates into between $19,000 – $66,000 per year in salary.

I think it's important to note, you should know who and what type of client you'd like to work with. We have all heard the term "riches are in niches", decide who you want to cater to. This can be small business owners, financial and tax professionals, real estate brokers, law firms, or medical offices.

In addition to becoming clear on who you'd like to work with, also think about what work you are willing to do. Don't go into this as a people pleaser or yes man. That is not what being a VA is about. I suggest focusing on 5 tasks or duties your agency will offer. Whether this is bookkeeping, customer service, social media management, personal errands, or lead generation. Know what you're good at, know what you'd like to offer, and don't stretch yourself too thin. As time goes on you'll naturally narrow down your offerings and also level up your skills to include some services that may pay more, like project management.

Let's say you want to focus solely on helping businesses with their social media. It'll be best to start a Social Media Agency. Social media management includes activities like posting text and image content, videos, and other content that drives audience engagement, as well as paid social media advertising.

New social media managers charge approximately $25 – $35 an hour to start, typically between 10 or 20 hours per month per client. This means that each client is worth $250 – $700 per month.

For example, I own a social media marketing agency iProfit Media Marketing, we offer marketing and management for Instagram and Facebook. One of our most popular packages include Facebook ad creation plus management monthly. We charge $1,000 a month. When I first launched this agency I signed on 10 clients, that's $10,000 a month literally just creating Facebook Ads, not including any of my other services. Tai Lopez, who's known to have one of the largest social media marketing agencies, says "If I had to start out again with no money or experience, I'd find small businesses to pay me up to $10,000 per month to manage their social media." Lopez estimates that the average customer will pay you $1,500 a month—even if you work part-time. Five clients conservatively make you $9,000 a month. That's a six-figure business.

To start you need to pick the right social media platform for your agency. Decide where you are strongest and where you have learned marketing strategies that work for yourself and others. Do you know how to help companies grow and leverage on YouTube, Pinterest, Facebook, Twitter, Linked In, or Twitter? Next, develop a tier of packages. For iProfit Marketing Media we have 3. Starting at $500 and scaling up to $2500 a month.

There are only 3 areas of focus on each platform.

✓ Postings
✓ Ads & Promotions
✓ Automations

We offer IG & Facebook because they are easily connected and that's where I have the most knowledge and strongest skill set. For our more established clients, I offer the 3rd area of focus which is email marketing automation. You are free to have add on services and customized packages for VIP clients, but make sure you have your core offerings structured in your business.

Next, you need to create your pricing. Please keep your business expenses in mind along with the ideal client's advertisement budget when creating pricing. After, focus on building your team. Again this is not freelancing it is an agency so at a minimum you'll need to have one assistant to help you delegate daily tasks and manage clients. You can also outsource some services, which is called "white labeling".

White labeling is a company that does digital marketing work for other digital marketing companies under their brand name.

To give you an example, I have 10 clients a month that have hired my agency to post on their Instagram page daily. I honestly don't have the time to do that all by myself. So I outsource. I'll hire a white labeling service that will post on my client's behalf for me. In the past, I've used 98 Buck Social for white labeling service.

Lastly, invest in the proper software and tech to manage clients and the business. Some form of client portal or project manager will be very helpful. I use Dubsado. I'm able to create clients profiles, send emails, send invoices, lead forms, schedule appointments, create contracts and questionnaires plus so much more. It offers so much and is easy to use. Use my code "dinasty" when signing up and receive 20% off.

Let's recap, here's what you'll need to do to start your agency:

1. Acquire the Necessary Skills.

2. Choose Your Niche.

3. Create your Menu of Services.

4. Determine Your Rates & Financial Policies.

5. Hire People to Help You.

6. Find Local Businesses As Your First Clients.

7. Collect Client Reviews and Testimonials.

The great thing about this type of business, VA's and SMM's can work from anywhere in the world. You no longer have to be in house to get these tasks done or get paid from them. Build your agency on your terms!

Dubsado | www.Dubsado.com
Business management solution designed to cut out the busywork.

Zirtual | www.Zirtual.com
Provides virtual assistant services to professionals, entrepreneurs, and small corporate teams.

98 Buck Social | www.98BuckSocial.com
works to support businesses big and small by maintaining a consistent presence on social media.

PLAN OF ACTION

" I will make $_____ in the next _____ months by selling _____ of _____ for $_____. "

NOTES:

_____

_____

_____

_____

_____

Braindump

Drop Shipping

Chapter 6: Drop Shipping

Definition - DropShipping
when a vendor fulfills orders from a third party and has them ship directly to the customer

Dropshipping has become a very popular and profitable way to start an online business. E-commerce and dropshipping profits have reached over $4 billion, which is a 7% a year on year increase for the last 10 years. I mean look around, the majority of the major retailers we shop with everyday use the drop-shipping model. This includes Wayfair, Amazon, and Walmart. But Amazon changed everything!

Amazon raised the bar by building warehouses everywhere, but not only that they come in with a competitive edge of having the fastest online shipping. You can dropship on Amazon through their Fulfilled by Amazon program. In this program, you ship your products to Amazon where they carry the inventory and ship directly to your customers. The average consumer expects to see a large assortment of items and to find the items they are looking for, all the while demanding faster shipping, free shipping, or both.

People are getting started selling and dropshipping on Amazon easily.

($) Set up an Amazon seller account.

($) Find a high-demand/low-competition product.

($) Check sites like Aliexpress for products

($) Create an Amazon listing.

E-commerce hosts have even noticed how popular this method is and integrated Amazon selling channels in their platform. Take Shopify for example, the Shopify app store allows you to use them to dropship from Amazon to your Shopify store. The "Amazon DropShipper" app has you login to Amazon and enter orders in.

Running an eCommerce business is much easier when you don't have to deal with physical products. Probably the biggest advantage of dropshipping is that it's possible to launch an e-commerce store without having to invest thousands of dollars in inventory upfront. You save time and money on things like office space or warehouse, packing and shipping orders, keeping track of inventory, handling returns, and hiring a fulfillment team. Because you don't have to deal with purchasing inventory or managing a warehouse, your overhead expenses are very low. Many successful dropshipping stores are run from home. A dropshipping business can be run from just about anywhere in the world with an internet connection. As long as you can communicate with suppliers and customers easily, you can run and manage your business. This can be from your phone or laptop.

Now still in 2020 dropshipping is a controversial subject. A lot of people get into it just for money and neglect basic business ethics. The reason some dropshipping stores are thriving while others aren't is that these dropshipping businesses keep customers first. They give priority to their buyers and try to solve all their needs. The key here is customer service. Don't focus solely on products and sales that you forget what's important. The people who are buying them. A proper e-commerce business needs to satisfy the customer. But when it comes to dropshipping business, we see that customers are often neglected for profit.

Also, don't list a product just because it's cheap. This is another big issue with dropshipping, the quality of products. Build a relationship with suppliers, and only work with those who are reliable and provide quality products

We hear the stories all the time, how people are making 6 to 7 figures from drop shipping. If that's your goal let's figure out how.

Let's say you get a product for $15 from AliExpress and you sell it for $30. After cutting the shipping costs and the cost of advertisements, your actual profit over the product is $10.

$10 profit x 1000 orders = $10,000 per month

$10,000 per month x 12 = $120,000 per year

So, if your goal of a successful dropshipping store is to earn $100,000 per year, then you need to sell at least 34 orders per day.

Don't get me wrong, this is not a get rich quick scheme. If you want to be successful in dropshipping, you will have to invest time, money, and effort. Personally, the people that I know who are killing it have these four major ingredients.

1 Invest in advertisements (Facebook & Google Adwords)

2 Sell high demand products at a competitive price

3 Prioritize professionalism

4 Great branding and some form of customer service.

Let's break this down and make it simple for you. Dropshipping is a retail fulfillment method where a store doesn't keep the products it sells in stock. Instead, when a store sells a product using the dropshipping model, it purchases the item from a third party and has it shipped directly to the customer. The customer places an order for the product, and after receiving payment for it, the seller places the same order with the supplier. Afterward, the supplier ships the product to the customer.

When done right, dropshipped items are fulfilled with the same branding, shipping performance, and customer experience as if they had come from the retailer's own warehouse, while allowing the retailer to take no inventory risk and enjoy wholesale margins.

Oberlo | www.Oberlo.com
Allows you to easily import products from suppliers directly into your Shopify store and ship directly to your customers

Aliexpress | www.Aliexpress.com
Online retailer with thousands of brands and millions of items at an incredible value

Amazon FBA | www.sell.amazon.com
a service provided by Amazon that provides storage, packaging, and shipping assistance to sellers.

Ebay | www.Ebay.com
Buy & sell electronics, cars, clothes, collectibles & more on eBay, the world's online marketplace.

PLAN OF ACTION

"

I will make $_____ in the next _____ months by selling _____ of _____ for $_____.

"

NOTES:

_____

_____

_____

_____

Braindump

Online Boutique

Chapter 7: Online Boutique

Definition - DropShipping
Online shopping is a form of electronic commerce which allows consumers to directly buy goods or services from a seller over the Internet using a web browser

The online selling market has been on the rise. Many are interested but don't know how to get started. This is where I got my start. My first business was an online hair boutique where I sold virgin hair extensions for hundreds of dollars. It was easy to set up, fun and gave me the first taste of my independence as a business owner. Online stores are the easiest way of selling products and you can capture a large number of customers easily with advancements of the internet and social media advertisement.

Unlike dropshipping, this does require more overhead, start-up fees, and a little groundwork, but everyone isn't looking for a quick way to do it. Let's say you want to be more hands-on. That's okay too and honestly, it makes the business better. For example, if you loved fashion your entire life and you always had a dream of owning a clothing line or boutique, the online boutique route would be the way to go.

Or you just had an amazing weight loss journey and lost over 50lbs and really have a passion to help others, a wellness and fitness store would be good for you. Also, another example, if you are a hairstylist or makeup artist that wants to create a beauty line for your clients, having an online boutique will be a great addition to your brand and an additional stream of income.

Selling apparel online is a very profitable business with a $90 billion yearly revenue. Statistics predict that the apparel and accessories online retail sector in the U.S. will generate about 138 billion dollars in revenue by 2022. Did you know Jeff Bezos owner of Amazon, created e-commerce In 1994? The first item ever was ordered online on Amazon was a book. And now over 20 years later, the e-commerce industry has made over 2 trillion US dollars in sales worldwide.

Starting an online boutique is more cost-effective than opening a brick-and-mortar store, but it's not cheap.

You don't have to lease commercial space or purchase a point-of-sale system, but your business will have some startup and operational costs such as inventory, marketing and branding material, plus website fees.

The first step of getting started is identifying the type of store you'd like to set up and conduct market research. Just as if you were starting a restaurant and looking into different locations, food options, and themes, you'll want to investigate the e-commerce area you're interested in and make some decisions concerning your specific business. Then you can choose a name and dive deeper into your branding. You'll want to choose a unique name, but one that also clearly indicates what your business is or does. Keep the customer first. Make sure everything appeals to your ideal audience.

Like a brick and mortar store, you'll need to register your online boutique and make sure you're operating legally. This will include obtaining a business license and permits, along with your EIN for the city or state.

Next, instead of searching for a location and preparing to set up your physical store, you'll start creating your website and online store. Like a physical storefront, this website will be the face of your business—it's what your customers will see first and what they'll use to browse and purchase your products or services. You want it to have curb appeal and attract a lot of foot traffic. Most e-commerce platforms not only allow you to create and launch your online store, but also customize your design, add your domain (or purchase one), manage inventory, take and ship orders, receive payment, and more.

Whether an all-in-one software, like Shopify or an open-source platform, like Magento, your e-commerce platform will be the base you use to build and develop your online store.

Once you've already done your research like mentioned above and you know what products you're going to sell, it's time make your products or source them from vendors and purchase wholesale. If you need help finding suppliers, multiple vendors and distributors visit my wholesale list at www.CoachedbyDinasty.com. Consider the inventory you want to start with, as well as what these startup costs will look like. Once finalized list all products in your online store.

Now that you have your products or services prepared and listed in your online store, your website is up and running, you're ready to start serving customers. To do this, of course, you'll need to properly market your online store. Sharing your business, or brand, across social media channels like Facebook, Instagram, Twitter, and Snapchat can be particularly useful when you're just starting your e-commerce operation. These kinds of early marketing are free and can be used to drop hints and build excitement about upcoming launches or product reveals.

These are the steps to starting an online boutique:

1. Research the e-commerce space and find your niche.

2. Select your business name and legal structure.

3. Apply for an employer identification number (EIN).

4. Choose an e-commerce platform and create your website.

5. Source or develop your products

6. Market your e-commerce business.

Because your business is based online, you can reach more potential customers, work from virtually anywhere and make money online without large overheads. Online is the place to be if you're looking to open a boutique or sell a product.

Many large retailers are closing their brick-and-mortar stores. In 2019, US retailers announced 9,302 store closings, a 59% jump from 2018, and the highest number since tracking the data began in 2012. More and more Americans are making purchases online. Consumers enjoy the freedom of shopping on their computer or phone and avoiding trips to a store that may not have had what they were looking for anyway.

RESOURCES

Shopify | www.Shopify.com
All the Ecommerce Tools You Need to Increase Sales & Improve Your Bottom Line.

Wix | www.Wix.com
Offers an excellent drag-and-drop site builder to create websites.

Paypal | www.Paypal.com
Worldwide online payment system that supports online money transfers.

Magento | www.Magento.com
Empowers thousands of retailers and brands with the best eCommerce platform.

Become a Boss Masterclass | www.become-a-boss.teachable.com
Learn How To Build A Successful Online Business In 30 Days.
Use code "BOSS" for $100 OFF

" I will make $_____ in the next ____ months by selling ____ of _____ for $_____. "

NOTES:

_____

_____

_____

_____

_____

_____

_____

Braindump

Network Marketing

Chapter 8: Network Marketing

Definition - Network Marketing

(Also known as multi-level marketing) is a business model that involves a pyramid structured network of people who sell a company's products.

Network marketing is one industry that has produced tons of millionaires. According to Les Brown, network marketing has created more millionaires than any industry around the world. USANA alone reports, as of 2017, around 400 USD millionaires and hundreds of thousands of "thousandaires". Some people become millionaires in as little as 3 years! As of now per the annual income reports of the year 2017-18, the richest person in network marketing is the dynamic duo Dexter and Birdie Yager of Amway International. They top the list with an annual income of $15.6 million.

This business model turns your everyday stay at home mom into the ultimate boss! At some point in life, you'll be introduced or a part of a network marketing business or purchase a product from someone who is. Thinking back on it my first experience was trying on my grandmother's Mary Kay products. I remember when I first got to college I met with a lady who tried to sign me up and sell me on Avon. I' m sure now you're thinking of all the times you have been exposed too.

I love the MLM business model! It's a mixture of dropshipping and affiliate marketing tied into one. You get the best of both worlds. The company in which you sign up under will handle customer service and ship all orders. It's your job to refer the product and business opportunity to close friends and colleagues.

So why does MLM get a bad rep? Let's be real, we have all heard it before oh it's a "scam" or "pyramid scheme". I believe MLM has been attacked with such negativity because many people enter with high hopes and unrealistic goals. Whether they have a bad sponsor who recruited them or they underestimated what was required of them and they have a poor work ethic. Either way, they sign up and don't get what they hope for so in return people bad mouth MLMs. I think Network Marketing is great, but it is hard work and takes a lot of commitment and consistency to be successful.

Let's get clear here, network marketing isn't a pyramid scheme. Pyramids are programs similar to chain letters where people just invest money based on the promise that other people will put in money that will filtrate back to them and somehow, they'll get rich.

A pyramid is strictly a money game and has no basis in real commerce. Normally, there's no product involved at all, just money changing hands.

Network marketing is a legitimate business. First, it's based on providing people with real, legitimate products they need and want at a fair price. While some people do make a lot of money through network marketing, their financial benefit is always the result of their own dedicated efforts in building an organization that sells real products and services. If you have what it takes and are willing to put in the work to build your business then this might be for you, keep reading.

How does network marketing really work? The participants in network marketing are usually compensated on a commission basis. That is, people in this network get commission every time they perform the specified task, like making a sale of a product, recruit a new team member or their recruits make a sale of the product. In simple words, this model involves a pyramid structure of non-salaried participants who get paid whenever they or a person below them in the network makes a sale.

There are different types of network marketing, before joining the business know which you are signing up for. **The three types include single-tier, two-tier, and multi-level.**

With single-tier network marketing, you sign up for a company's affiliate program to sell their products or services. You do not need to recruit other distributors, and all your pay comes from direct sales. Avon, the popular beauty company, uses single-tier networking marketing.

Two-tier network marketing does involve some recruiting, but your pay isn't solely dependent on it. You get paid for direct sales (or traffic you drive to a website) and for direct sales or referred traffic made by affiliates or distributors you recruit to work under you. An example of a two-tier program is Ken Envoy's Site Sell.

Multi-Level Marketing (MLM) is a distribution-based marketing network that contains two or more tiers. Two other types of network marketing strategies are marketing-driven networks and name-driven network marketing. Some MLM programs allow you to make money five or more tiers deep, so there may be incentives for recruiting. Examples of MLM businesses include LuLaRoe, Magnetic Sponsoring, and Amway.

The key to be successful in these types of companies is to hire people excited about the product or opportunity to work with you. Marketing is part industry-driven and part creative thinking. With network marketing, it is also about finding salespeople with enthusiasm.

When you hire people who are excited about your business and product, they will share that enthusiasm with others. An enthusiastic salesforce leads to more sales and recruits into your marketing network.

The future with network marketing business is strong and should be considered as a serious career and earning opportunity. Network Marketing is a business in which we don't invest a lot of money, but we invest time. With network marketing, there are no big capital requirements, no location limitations, no minimum quotas required, and no special education or skills needed. Network marketing is a low-overhead, home-based business that can actually offer many of the advantages associated with owning your own business. Network marketing is a people-to-people business that can significantly expand your circle of friends. It's a business that enables you to travel and have fun as well as enjoy the lifestyle that extra income can provide.

Get started with network marketing:

1 Find a Company With a Product You Love.

2 Be Genuine and Ethical.

3 Identify Your Target Market.

4 Set a Specific Goal.

5 Surround Yourself with Successful Leaders and Coaches.

6 Invite Two People daily to Look at the Opportunity.

RESOURCES

Network Marketing Secrets | www.networkmarketingsecrets.com
How To Use Sales Funnels To Grow Your Network Marketing Business

Go Pro | www.networkmarketingpro.com
7 Steps to Becoming a Network Marketing Professional.

MLM I recommend are TLC, Herbalife, Le-vel and Beach Bod

" I will make $_____ in the next ____ months by selling ____ of _____ for $_____. "

NOTES:

_____

_____

_____

_____

_____

_____

_____

Braindump

Brand Ambassador

Chapter 9: Brand Ambassador

Definition - Network Marketing
a person who is paid to endorse or promote a particular company's products or services.

A few years ago being a brand ambassador was a career solely for celebrities, models, or people of status. Social media has leveled the playing field. That girl you went to high school with or the kid you use to babysit is now being paid to represent brands and companies. Some people prefer the phrase, "influencer", and still reserve brand ambassadors for celebrity or people in long term contracts with a company for promotion. For the sake of this chapter, I'll be using both terms interchangeably.Brand ambassadors are simply people who represent and talk about a company positively, preferably in front of lots of potential customers and get paid. They promote a brand and its products to their network to increase brand awareness and help drive sales.

The average influencer can take home anywhere from $30,000 to $100,000 per year by promoting products like clothing, food, hotels and even vitamin supplements on their pages. Users with more than 1 million followers can make more than $100,000, or even up to $250,000, per sponsored post, according to a 2018 Vox report.The easiest platforms to leverage is YouTube and Instagram. Some of the biggest non-celebrity influencers often gained their first taste of exposure on these platforms. This is basically a business where you brand yourself, you are the product, and brands pay you to drive awareness and revenue.

Building a personal brand can help you make a lot of money online. Did you know in 2018, Kylie Jenner made $1 million for every sponsored Instagram post, making her the highest-paid influencer? While it may seem like reality stars, singers, and athletes are the biggest influencers, keep in mind that even smaller-scale influencers can make more money today than they did a year ago. This especially has held true as buyers and consumers turn to social media platforms to research and see what friends, family, and colleagues are recommending.

To make money as an influencer, you can charge for sponsored posts, speaking gigs, create your own online store and sell products, add affiliate links in your bio, sell your photos, sell ads on a podcast, get paid as a brand ambassador, create a book, get paid to appear at events, and more. If you have a website or a large social media following, you can also make money by pursuing sponsored posts and ads. But, how does this work?

Companies are willing to pay bloggers and social media influencers to promote their products and services. If you have a platform, be it a blog or a huge Instagram following, you can cash in.There are different types of influencers, don't worry you don't have to be the next Kardashian to make a living as a brand ambassador.

The 4 Types of Influencers are Mega, Macro, Micro, and Nano.

Mega Influencers are A-list celebrities on social media and in real life. Their following spans over 10M typically and they charge hundreds of thousands to millions for a post. Macro influencers are similar to mega influencers, with the main difference being macro-influencers usually rise to fame through the web, as opposed to the genuine celebrities that make up mega influencers. Macro influencers can be podcasters, vloggers, social media stars, and influential bloggers. Their audience size would normally be between 100,000 and a million followers and they can charge anywhere between $10,000-$50,000 per post.

Micro influencer's audience ranges from 1,000 to 100,000 followers – however, while their audience may be smaller, they're more invested in their audience and their niche. Micro-influencers can make as much as a few thousand dollars per post ranging from $500-$2500.

Micro-influencers are respected because of their expertise on a topic they usually stick to one topic and leverage their knowledge to build their thought leadership.

A nano-influencer is defined as an Instagram influencer with between 1,000 and 10,000 followers. Nano-influencers' audiences are small, niche, and highly engaged. They can charge an average of $100-$300 per post. Nano-influencers have the smallest following of all tiers of influencers, but many times make the best content because they're passionate.

Brand ambassadors not only get paid flat rates, but companies also send them free stuff or negotiate in the percentage of sales for campaigns. I remember the first time I received payment to do a sponsored post for a fashion boutique, I was shocked on how easy it was to make money. The owner paid me $500 for one Instagram photo and one YouTube video, I only had around 30,000 followers at the time. It was fun being able to receive new clothes, dress up all cute and being paid to post. I've also received numerous free items on companies or clients behalf, and I'll give them a shout out or review. It's real money and benefits in influencer marketing, Instagram and YouTube seems to be the two platforms you can make the most cash.

The highest-paid YouTuber is 7-year-old Ryan, who reviews toys on his YouTube channel which made him $22 million in 2018.

There are a ton of YouTube channels out there on any topic you can think of, and most of the people with a big following are earning some money in exchange for their videos and time. The secret to making money on YouTube is to create content people want that either educates or entertains. You can use a headline that's clickbait to entice people to watch or you can use keywords that are optimized for YouTube search. Once you've reached the 1,000-subscriber milestone, you can officially monetize your channel with YouTube ads.

Every time someone sees an ad on your videos, it counts toward your account. At 10,000 views, the potential to get paid truly begins. With every 10,000 clicks, your number goes up. "Cost per impression" is the metric YouTube uses to gauge how much to pay you, also known as CPI.

Your YouTube channel should focus on a single niche so you can build a strong, loyal audience. For example, you can create makeup tutorials, stream video games, review products, teach skills, create prank videos, or anything else you think there'd be an audience for.

Here's my best advice if you want to be a brand ambassador and take it seriously, first you need to take your content seriously. Produce quality and consistent content. There are tons of videos out there about how to take professional-quality photos on your iPhone or camera, and other influencers have tips as well on how to edit your photos. If you purchased the e-course along with this book, I'll be showing you more examples along with tips and tricks in the course. Also, build a real and strong relationship with your following. You have to show up, remember your job is literally to be a source for them, referring them to different products and services, they have to trust you. The more results and sales you bring the brands the more they'll pay you.

Here are some action steps. Make a list of 10-20 brands you'll like to work with, understand what you offer and how your audience correlates with their company. Make yourself a professional Media Kit, Canva has a lot of templates, and begin to email or DM to pitch yourself. This week alone I received 7 brand partnerships or new affiliate relationships by doing those exact steps. I set out to feature multiple companies in this book, and I used my influence to do so. It works! Invest in yourself, your content, be consistent, and do the work.

Get started as an Brand Ambassador:

1. Identify Your Niche.

2. Pick Your Platform.

3. Prioritize Your Content.

4. Maintain Consistency.

5. Collaborate with Other Influencers.

6. Create and Post Relevant Content.

7 Up Your Hashtag Game.

8 Engage With Your Audience.

9 Let Brands Know You're Open to Collaborations.

RESOURCES

Famebit | www.Famebit.com
Leading self-service influencer marketing platform where brands and influential creators collaborate for branded content endorsements.

Upfluence | www.Upfluence.com
The best influencer platform to help you scale your influencer marketing campaigns

The Influencer League | www.TheInfluencerLeague.com
The Ivy League for Influencers.

" I will make $_____ in the next
____ months by selling ____ of
_____ for $_____. "

NOTES:

_____

_____

_____

_____

_____

_____

_____

Braindump

Websites That Pay

Chapter 10: Websites That Pay

Definition - Websites That Pay
legitimate ways to make money online from websites that pay you for service or products

Throughout the book, I have given you several different business ideas you can start to make money online and work from home. Let's say you are not interested in owning your own business and you just want ways to make extra money. Well, you're in luck, I haven't forgot about you!

There are several websites that pay and ways you can make money online without setting up an entire business model or having to be tech-savvy. We can start with some companies that will allow you to work from home.

If you're interested in working for someone else, while still making your own schedule, here are a few companies that will let you do just that. LiveOps is a call center that allows you to work from home. Once you're set up to take the calls, you can begin making a weekly schedule and working from home. The pay is generally close to $10/hour, but you can earn more with commissions.

Fast Chart allows you to work from home as a medical transcriptionist. There are some requirements and qualifications, but if you meet them, you'll make competitive pay for the industry. You'll also be able to set your own schedule since you'll be working from home. SpeakWrite will pay you up to $15/hour to transcribe information. You set your schedule and work from home.

Your opinion matters and you can also get paid by taking surveys online. It's easy to earn cash for surveys. How much you get paid completely depends on the number of surveys you attempt and complete and the amount of time it takes to complete a survey. Each online survey has a different payout, with some offering as much as $50. With over 20 million active members, Swagbucks is one of the best-paid survey sites for survey takers to make money for giving their opinion online. Swagbucks provides access to tens of thousands of paid survey-taking opportunities with new surveys added every day.

Harris Poll is run by the Nielsen Group, making them part of one of the largest and most respected market research firms in the country. At Harris Poll, you will be provided the opportunity to fill out surveys for some household brands, and earn rewards from companies like Amazon, ESPN, iTunes, The Wallstreet Journal, and Starbucks.

With Inbox Dollars, you can earn money for a lot more than just taking surveys. If you opt-in, you can also earn money for reading emails, and letting Inbox Dollars learn about you as you shop online and play online games.

Cash Crate is another option that pays for a variety of activities, including surveys, playing games online and getting paid for web searches. Unlike many other programs, Cash Crate is happy to send you a check – not just a gift card – for your earnings once per month.

Do you have a bunch of old items or things you no longer use in your house? Most of us do. Did you know you can make money from them just by posting online? Create a listing, make a PayPal account to accept payments, take some nice quality photos and go live! Places like Facebook Marketplace, Mercari, LetGo, Craigslist, and OfferUp are a quick start. Gary Vee preaches this method all the time. He still goes to garage sales and thrift stores to spruce items he can "flip", mark up, and sell online for a profit. I'm going to give you another little tip for a BIG payday. Visit outlets or last call stores. Such as Dillard's or Macy's going out of business, Nordstrom Rack or Neiman Marcus Last Call. Let's say it's your lucky day and you come across a Gucci sweater marked down 50%-70% retail price. Brand new, mint condition, you'll definitely be able to markup and sell that item online or even to consignment shops.

If you like to create arts and crafts, you can sell them on Etsy. It's completely free to open an Etsy store. You simply sign up, post pictures of your creations and start selling.

Most people have more clothes in their closet than they ever wear. You likely have items you haven't worn in the past year that you never have any intention of wearing ever again. Whether you sell your clothes, handbags, or shoes there are quite a few websites that allow you to sell your used fashion items. Poshmark, Refashioner, TheRealReal, ThredUp, and Tradesy are a few of the online sites where you can sell your used apparel.

Poshmark is a digital buying and selling marketplace for fashion that has more than 5,000 brands for sale from sellers just like you. It's women like Jenna Naschek, a 33-year-old Atlantan who has turned her Poshmark reselling side hobby into a full-fledged, full-time, six-figure business.

You could make money online by selling on several different platforms. If you're looking to sell items in person, you can use Facebook buy and sell groups in your community to find people online and sell the items in person. I've personally sold in these groups before and know they work.

"I will make $_____ in the next ____ months by selling ____ of _____ for $_____"

NOTES:

_____

_____

_____

_____

_____

_____

_____

_____

Braindump

Conclusion

Conclusion

I've been making money online since I was 18 years old, I'm 25 now and it is still my main source of income and favorite thing to do. This book is only the beginning! It's here to plant the seed and provide you with the resources.

Now it's time for you to believe in yourself and go do the work!

I've done it, so I know it's possible and my bank account plus tax statements show proof of that. Deciding to start making money online has blessed me to be able to travel all over the world, purchase my dream car, pay student loans debt, live in an amazing high-rise condo, help my family when they're in need but most of all not to worry. Most of my bills are set on auto-pay and I never have that fear of if they'll be covered or not or when a withdraw comes out of my account will I go in the negative.

I highly suggest, if you haven't and you're serious about learning how to take your online business to this level of success sign up for the digital e-course that comes along with this book. You can find it at www.CoachedbyDinasty.com. We will dive deeper and I'll be able to show you real examples, how-to's, and bank statements on how I've been able to make money online.

I suggest whatever route you decide to take from this book, pick one and focus on it for the next 90 days. Take a week to research, google more information, watch YouTube Videos, find experts in your field you can learn from and so on. Invest and educate yourself as much as possible so that you can be the best at what you do.

There's a ridiculous number of ways to make money online and what I've covered here is just the tip of the iceberg. If you have time, a passion for almost anything, and at least some creative skill, you'll be able to build an online income stream — or several.

Be consistent, that's most important and give yourself time to grow. You'll see your online business flourish right before your eyes.

Making money online can help you earn some extra side hustle cash but it can also help you escape your 9 to 5 job so you can become a full-time entrepreneur. By making more money, you gain more financial freedom, improve your financial security, and inch closer to living life on your terms. It's possible to earn a living online if you work hard and stick with it.

But, don't just take my word for it. If you look online, you'll find thousands of success stories you can use for inspiration.

So, which stream of income will you try out first?

♡ *Dinasty*

www.ingramcontent.com/pod-product-compliance
Lightning Source LLC
Chambersburg PA
CBHW041703200326
41518CB00002B/171